STORIES FROM ANCIENT ROME

The son of "Manlius Torquatus, provoked beyond endurance by the taunts of the Latin champion, rode out from the ranks."

STORIES FROM ANCIENT ROME

BY

PROF. A. J. CHURCH, M. A.

*with FRONTISPIECE, SEVEN DRAWINGS
BY H. R. MILLAR, AND MANY OTHER
ILLUSTRATIONS*

YESTERDAY'S CLASSICS

CHAPEL HILL, NORTH CAROLINA

This edition, first published in 2006 by Yesterday's Classics, is an unabridged republication of the work originally published by Funk & Wagnalls Company in 1907. For a complete listing of the books published by Yesterday's Classics, please visit the website www.yesterdaysclassics.com. Yesterday's Classics is the publishing arm of the Baldwin Project which presents the complete text of dozens of classic books for children at www.mainlesson.com under the editorship of Lisa M. Ripperton and T. A. Roth.

ISBN-10: 1-59915-061-1

ISBN-13: 978-1-59915-061-1

Yesterday's Classics
PO Box 3418
Chapel Hill, NC 27515

CONTENTS

Page

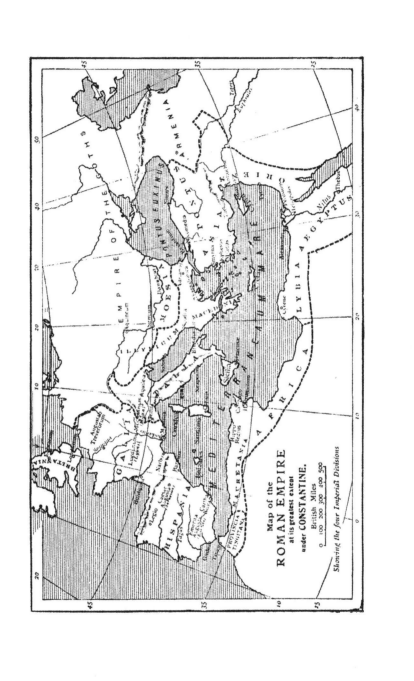

Map of the
ROMAN EMPIRE
at its greatest extent
under CONSTANTINE.
British Miles
0 100 200 300 400 500

Showing the four Imperial Divisions

CHAPTER I

THE BEGINNINGS OF A STATE

ABOUT the middle of the eighth century before Christ, there was founded in Italy a new town which was to become the most famous in the world. The site of Rome, for that was the name of the new foundation, was very well chosen. A number of hills—they were reckoned as seven, though there were not so many separate heights—looked down upon a riverside meadow. The hills were steep enough to be easily defended, but not too steep to be built upon.

The river was navigable, and the distance from the sea was not so great as to cause inconvenience, but was enough to make the town safe from the attacks of pirates. The first settlers occupied two of the seven hills, one of the two being certainly the Palatine, the other probably the Quirinal. They seem to have been shepherds or herdsmen. So much we may gather from the oldest names, such, for instance, as that of one of the gates in the first city wall, *Porta mugionis*, "the gate of lowing."

One of the reasons which probably brought about the settlement at Rome was the fact that the country to the south was troubled by eruptions from a volcano. There is, it is true, no volcano now, but the lake of Alba, a town of which I shall soon have to speak, has evidently been at some time a crater. Some settlers may have been fugitives from neighbouring towns, men who had broken the laws and were flying from justice, or who had been driven out by civil strife.

Whoever the inhabitants of the new town may have been or wherever they may have come from, there very soon arose a difficulty which is felt in all young settlements, as in our own colonies in times past or even now—where were they to find wives? The chief of Rome sent envoys to the neighbouring towns, belonging to two peoples known as Latins and Sabines, and asked that the Roman townsfolk might be allowed to intermarry with them.

Rome was not, however, well liked among its neighbours. If its population was partly made up of people who had got into trouble at home, there was good reason why they should not be regarded with favour. At any rate the envoys were not well received, and their request was refused. The Romans then resolved to get by force what they could not persuade their neighbours to give them.

Romulus—who was their chief—proclaimed a great festival, to which, in the name of his people, he invited the inhabitants of the neighbouring towns, together with their wives and daughters. They came in great numbers.

While the guests were looking on at the games, which, as usual, were a part of the festival, the young men of Rome rushed in among them and carried off the unmarried women. The men, unprepared and un-armed as they were, could make no resistance. All that they were able to do was to make their own escape.

Of course the angry towns resolved to punish the Romans for this outrage; and if they had combined in an attack on the new State, they would very probably have conquered it. But they were too angry to wait. Even the three Latin towns which had suffered most did not act together. Separately they attacked the Roman territory, and separately they were beaten. One of them was glad to accept the terms which Romulus offered, and was united with Rome.

But when the great Sabine people, under its king, Titus Tatius, advanced to the attack, the danger became serious. The Romans did not venture to meet this powerful enemy in the field, but prepared to defend their walls. But the walls did not sufficiently protect them. The Sabines gained possession of the citadel, by the treachery of a woman, as the Romans declared—they were always ready to account for any-thing that was not to their credit. However this may have been, the invaders certainly made their way into the city. There the fighting was furious.

At first the Sabines had the best of it, and the Romans fled. Romulus vowed to build a temple to Jupiter the Stayer, if the flight was stopped. His prayer was answered—so runs the story—the Romans turned fiercely upon their pursuers, and these in their turn fell back. Then came another change; the Sabines rallied, and the Romans could do little more than hold their own.

"In a pause of battle the Sabine women rushed
between the hostile lines."

In a pause of the battle the Sabine women rushed between the hostile lines, some of them carrying in their arms the children whom they had borne to their Roman husbands. They begged of their fathers and brothers on the one side and their husbands on the other, to cease from a strife from which, however it might end, they were bound to suffer. Their entreaties were heard. The battle was stopped; terms of peace were discussed, and in the end the two nations were made into one, under the joint rule of Romulus and Tatius.

Before long Tatius met his death in a private quarrel, and Romulus reigned alone for the rest of his life. His successor, Numa, a Sabine, it would seem, by birth, was a man of peace. His long reign of forty-one years was given to the ordering of religion and law. The two peoples which had been brought together in so strange a way were made into one harmonious whole.

Much might be said of the things that go to prove this union, but it will suffice to mention, as long as the Roman State lasted its citizens were wont to be called by the name of *Quirites*, the very namewhich the Sabine kings of old had used in addressing their subjects.

The reign of Tullus Hostilius, the warrior-king who succeeded the peaceful Numa, brought another accession to the State of Rome. Some twelve miles to the south stood the ancient city of Alba Longa. Between this city and Rome there was a close tie of kindred. Romulus was the grandson of an Alban king, the son of a princess who had been ill-treated by a usurping uncle, and some at least of his subjects in the new city which he had founded had been of Alban birth.

But kinship does not always mean friendship. The Jews, for instance, owned the relationship of nations for which they felt the bitterest hatred, Edom, Midian, Moab and Ammon. So it was with Alba and Rome. There were often border wars between the two States. Out of these was developed in course of time a serious struggle which could but end in the overthrow of one or the other.

The army of Alba invaded the Roman territory under its king, this monarch fell in battle, and the army retreated within their own borders. The Romans followed them, and a great battle seemed certain, when the Alban general proposed that the quarrel should be fought out by champions chosen from the two sides. The champions of Rome were three brothers of the name of Horatius; those of Alba three Curiatii.

In the conflict that followed two of the Horatii were killed; the third remained unhurt. None of the Alban champions had fallen, but they were all wounded. The surviving Roman contrived to separate them, and was more than a match for each taken by himself. In the end they all fell by his hand.

The army of Alba was now, according to the agreement, at the disposal of the Roman king, and he had soon occasion for its services. One of the most powerful of the Latin cities, which had been for some time in subjection to Rome, made an alliance with the

Etruscan city of Veii, and on the strength of it declared its independence.

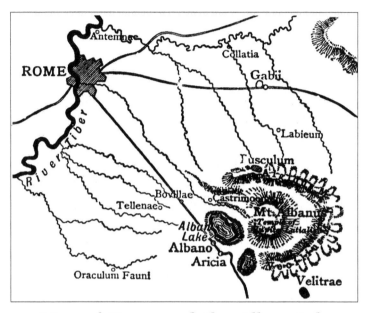

Map of Rome and the Alban Lake

The Roman king summoned the army of Alba to his help. It obeyed, so far as to appear on the field of battle, but it took no part in the struggle. It awaited the result. When victory declared for the Romans, the Alban general came up and offered his congratulations. But the Roman king was not disposed to submit to such treatment. He seized the Alban general, and ordered his body to be fastened to two chariots; they were then driven in different directions, and the unhappy man was torn asunder. This revenge was followed up by destroying the city of Alba and transferring the whole of its population to Rome. Thus did

7

Rome within little more than a century from its foundation absorb two considerable peoples.

It is very likely that other great powers, such as the mighty monarchies of the East, have had much the same beginning. But there is an incident in the story of how Rome got the upper hand of Alba which seems to mark the character of the new State. When the victorious Horatius was coming back to Rome, escorted by his comrades, and carrying the spoils of the vanquished champions, the women went forth to meet him, and among them was his sister. She spied among the trophies of the victory a garment which she had made for her betrothed, an Alban youth, and she burst into loud cries of sorrow. This untimely grief stirred his wrath, and he struck her to the ground.

He was tried for the crime upon the spot, condemned—for, indeed, his guilt was obvious—and sentenced to death. As the officers of justice were binding him, that he might undergo his sentence to be scourged and then hanged, the young man cried: "I appeal to the people." And his cause was tried again before a general assembly. This remitted the penalty upon condition that certain rites of humiliation should be undergone.

It was a sign that the new power, which was to have so great an influence on the history of the world, was to be a rule of law administered by a free people.

CHAPTER II

A LIFE AND DEATH STRUGGLE

THE year 510 was a year of revolution in Southern Europe, as in modern times was 1848. It was then that Athens drove out the sons of Pisistratus; it was then that Rome expelled the House of Tarquin. The first Tarquin was an Etrurian noble who had come to Rome at some time in the reign of its fourth king, Ancus Martius. He had become famous there by his wealth and great talents, and had somehow contrived to secure the succession to the throne. Rome had prospered under his rule, and though, after his death, the royal power passed for a while out of his family, the name of Tarquin was still a power in the State.

By help of this, by Etruscan influence, for the Etruscans were near neighbours of Rome, their great city of Veii being but ten miles distant, and by his own daring, the grandson of the first Tarquin became the seventh King of Rome—and the last. It is needless to tell the story of how and why he was expelled.

Though his rule was oppressive, he was able and successful. Rome became the acknowledged chief of the Latin cities; her territory was enlarged at the expense of her neighbours, the Volsci; she had the

9

advantage of being on friendly terms with the Etrurians.

It was the bad conduct of one of his sons that caused the king's overthrow and exile. The Romans' latest experience of monarchy made them resolve to change their form of government.

Theirs was to be a free State, though much was to be done and suffered, as we shall see, before freedom was reached. There were to be two heads of the State, who should hold office for a year; they were to be called *Prætors* (foremost men), a title which was changed before long into *Consuls* (colleagues).

The expelled monarch was not disposed to accept the new order of things, and he lost no time in attempting to recover his throne. He had not, as had his fellow-sufferer in Greece, the son of Pisistratus, to wait for the slow movements of an Eastern king, who was hundreds of miles away.* His friends were at hand, for it was, of course, to the Etrurians that he appealed for help.

His first effort, however, was made in another direction. He had friends and helpers at Rome, some who really believed that the old order of things was better than the new, and others who had profited by the royal favour in the past, and looked to profit by it in the future. Tarquin sent envoys to Rome; they were nominally to ask that his private property should be restored to him, really to communicate with a royalist party which had conspired to restore the king to his

---

* Hippias, the son of Pisistratus, was expelled in 510. It was not until 490 that the Persians made a real effort to restore him.

throne. The conspiracy was discovered, however, and it was punished in a way which showed how sternly resolved the chiefs of the new Republic could be to do their duty without fear or favour.

Among the guilty were the two sons of Lucius Junius Brutus, who was one of the recently appointed prætors or consuls. Brutus made no attempt to save his sons from the penalty of their crime. On the contrary, he presided at their trial, pronounced on them the sentence of death, and sat with unmoved countenance while they were scourged and beheaded.

As for the property of the banished family, it was divided among the people, who were thus bound more strongly to support the new order of things.

Not long after, the Roman army met the allies of Tarquin in the field. Before the battle began, Brutus and one of the sons of Tarquin met in single combat. Both were slain. The battle itself had no decisive result, but Tarquin certainly was no nearer than before to recovering his throne.

In the course of the following year, however, he found a more powerful friend. This was Lars Porsena, King of Clusium, and head of the great league of Etrurian cities. The Romans did not venture to meet their new enemy in the field, and they failed to hold their first line of defence. This was the Janiculum Hill on the right or Etrurian bank of the Tiber—Lars Porsena took it by storm.

Rome itself now seemed to be at his mercy, for he had only to cross the bridge which joined the Jani-

"Horatius held his place till the
structure had actually fallen."

culum to the city. But here he was baffled by the bold-ness of three heroic Romans. The three, representing the three great elements in the Roman people, Latin, Sabine, and Etrurian, held the bridge till its supports were cut away, and the river thus rendered impassable. The names of all, Spurius Lartius, Titus Herminius, and Horatius Cocles (Cocles means the One-Eyed), lived for ever in the memories of their countrymen, but the third was held in especial honour. His two comrades retreated to the Roman side while the last supports of the bridge were still standing; Horatius held his place till the structure had actually fallen. Then, weakened as he was by wounds, and burdened with the weight of his armour, he leapt into the river and just succeeded in reaching the Roman bank.

Rome was safe for the time, but the prospect of the future was dark. Lars Porsena had practically command of the whole country; the food supplies were cut off, and the city, which was crowded with fu-gitives from the rural districts, was in danger of starva-tion.

A young Roman noble, Caius Mucius by name, thought of a plan, which he told to a number of his friends, of delivering his country by getting rid of its powerful enemy. He made his way into the Etrurian camp, to all appearance unarmed, but carrying a dagger concealed about his person.

The King's secretary was seated in a conspicu-ous place, busy in receiving applications and petitions. He was clad in a splendid robe of purple, and Mucius, thinking him to be the King, stabbed him to the heart.

He was at once seized and taken before Porsena. The King threatened him with torture. Mucius replied by thrusting his right hand into the fire, which was burning hard by, and holding it there till it was consumed.

"I am not afraid of your tortures," he said, "still I will tell you the secret which you wish to extort from me. Know, then, that there are three hundred men who are as determined as I am to rid the country of its most dangerous enemy. One by one they will make the attempt, and you may feel sure that sooner or later they will succeed."

The King was so impressed with this threat that he resolved to come to terms with so determined an enemy. So he made a proposal for a treaty, and as he was willing to give up his demand that King Tarquin should be restored to his throne, the Romans gladly accepted his terms.

He was to have yet another proof of how bold a race he had to deal with. Hostages, ten boys and as many girls, were handed over to him, to be held in custody till the conditions should be fulfilled; but Clœlia, one of the girl-hostages, contrived to elude the soldiers who were guarding her, and plunged into the river. Her companions followed her example, and all reached the Roman bank in safety. The Romans, however, sent them back, and Porsena, greatly impressed by this display of courage and good faith, set the hostages at liberty, restored without ransom all the prisoners whom he had captured, and even handed over to the besieged for the relief of their distress all the stores in his camp.

These picturesque stories must not, however, hide from us the truth that Rome had, in fact, to undergo a great humiliation. One Roman writer tells us that the city was surrendered to Porsena; another informs us that among the terms of the treaty was one frequently imposed upon a conquered people—as by Sisera on the Hebrews in the days of Deborah and Barak, and by the Philistines in the time of Saul—that no iron should be used except for agricultural tools.

One more great struggle Rome had to make before her freedom was assured, and this was with her Latin kinsfolk. One of the most powerful of the Latin chiefs was Octavius Mamilius, of Tusculum, who had married a daughter of King Tarquin. The decisive battle took place at the Lake Regillus.

There we hear, for the first time, of a personage who often appears in Roman history. The consuls were superseded for a time, and a dictator whose power was absolute took their place.

One of the old champions of the bridge reappeared and slew the Latin chief. Other deeds of valour were performed; Rome was helped, so the story ran, by the presence of the twin brethren, Castor and Pollux, just as in Spanish history we hear of St. James of Compostella leading on the Christian army against the Moors. In the end the Latin army was routed. This was in 495, and two years later Tarquin died.

The city of Veii, one of the most ancient and most formidable of the enemies of Rome, seems to have taken no part in the campaigns of Porsena. This king represented an adverse party in the Etruscan

15

League. We even find him, when he had become friendly to the Romans, gratifying them by a gift of Veientine territory. When we remember that Veii was only twelve miles distant from Rome—less than the distance that Kingston-upon-Thames is from London—we perceive what a fortunate circumstance this was. After the death of Porsena the two cities were constantly at war. It is impossible to do more than note one or two of the principal events. In 476 happened the great disaster of Cremera. It is a strange story. The Veientines, unable to withstand the Roman army in the field, took shelter within their walls, issuing forth when occasion offered to plunder and destroy.

One of the great Roman families, the Fabii, undertook to deal with the trouble. It should be their business to protect their country against these robbers. The whole clan—three hundred and six men, not one of whom, says Livy, the Senate would have deemed unfit for high command—marched out of Rome, and took up a position which commanded the hostile territory. This they held for two years with success; in the third they were lured into an ambush, and perished to a man.

Only one young lad of the Fabian race remained. Happily, he had been left in Rome, for he was to be the ancestor of a race which was to serve the country in after times. Twenty years after this the Romans determined to put an end to the perpetual annoyance of an enemy almost at their gates. They found it no easy task, even though Veii received no help from the other Etruscan cities. The siege lasted for ten years, a period of supreme importance in the history of Rome, because she then had for the first time a standing army. In the tenth year a strange phenomenon was observed. The Alban Lake rose so high as to threaten the surrounding country.

The oracle of Delphi being consulted directed that the waters should be drained off, not by the usual channel, but by distributing them over the country, and that this would bring about the capture of the city. This may mean that by making a new outlet the means of driving a mine under Veii was discovered. This seems to have been the way in which the city was taken. A band of Roman soldiers suddenly emerged in the temple of Juno, which stood on the citadel. The inhabitants made a fierce resistance, but after a while, under a promise of their lives, laid down their arms. They were sold into slavery. In such matters the age had no scruples, but the gods of the place could not be disposed of so easily. A pius excuse was therefore invented. Juno was the patron deity of the city, and one of those who had been commissioned to deal with the matter asked her "either," says Livy, "by inspiration or in jest," whether she was willing to go to Rome. Her associates declared that the image nodded assent; some went so far as to say that they heard the words, "I am willing." For some years Veii stood empty; more than once Roman citizens, discontented with their lot at home, took up their abode in it. Once at least a general migration was proposed. But there was no permanent settlement. The place fell into decay. Three centuries and a half later Propertius sang:—

"O ancient Veii! splendid once and great,
  Her forum graced with throne of royal state;
  Now there the lazy shepherd's horn is blown,
  And where her chiefs lie dead the harvest mown."

CHAPTER III

A BLOODLESS REVOLUTION

DEBT is, and always has been, a great difficulty in a people's life. It is impossible to carry on business without borrowing or lending money, but trouble is continually arising out of it.

There are in England at the present time thousands of cases every year of people who either will not or cannot pay what they owe. Some borrow with reasonable hopes of repaying and fail in their ventures; some do not think much about what they are doing, but get the money because they want or fancy that they want the things which may be bought with it; some deliberately deceive their creditors and borrow because they will not work.

In ancient times, and in England up to quite recently, the laws about debtors were very severe. Nowhere were they more severe than in Rome. When a man owed money and had no property which could be taken and applied in payment, he might himself be seized and put into what was called an *ergastulum* or workhouse and compelled to labour for the benefit of his creditors. There was even a provision in the law that his creditors might, if they thought fit, take his body and cut it up into pieces and so satisfy at least their revenge. It is said, however, that this provision was never actually carried out.

The law was very severe; many suffered by it, and were reduced to a condition very like slavery. The debtor was not actually a slave, for he could regain his freedom by paying what he owed; but till that was done a slave he practically was.

When times were hard, when the harvest was bad or the country wasted by war, this debt trouble became very serious. It is not surprising, therefore, to find that about fifteen years after the expulsion of the Kings, when Rome had been doing all she could to defend herself against many enemies, it came to a head.

This year there was a quarrel with the Volscians, and an army had to be raised to meet them in the field. It will be remembered that there was no standing army in those days; soldiers were enlisted when they were wanted.

The Forum or public square of the city where the consuls were sitting to receive the names of recruits, was crowded with people, when a man who had often served and had risen to the rank of centurion,[*] appeared in its midst. He had been put into an *ergastulum* by his creditor, and had been there treated most cruelly. He showed the marks left by the scourge and the hot iron, while at the same time he could point to the honourable scars of wounds received in the service of his country. It was no fault of his, he declared, that

---

[*] The commander of a century of one hundred men, a rank corresponding to that of captain in the British army.

he had failed to pay his debt. His farm had been laid waste, his cattle driven off by Sabine raiders.

The indignation of the people rose high; some of the workhouses were broken open and their inmates set free; senators and others who had the reputation of dealing harshly with their debtors were assaulted. No names were given to the consuls. But when tidings reached the city that the enemy were approaching, better thoughts prevailed, the more readily because some concessions were made; the chief of these was that no proceedings were to be taken against a debtor while he was serving in the field. When the fighting was over, there was a return to the old state of things.

Unfortunately, one of the consuls now elected belonged to the Claudian family, whose traditional policy it was to set themselves against popular liberties, and the following year the quarrel broke out again with even more violence than before. The people flatly refused to enlist, and this though the Volscians had actively taken the field. The Senate had recourse to a measure reserved for great emergencies and appointed a dictator.[*]

The partisans of Claudius endeavoured to secure this office for him, but, happily, were not successful. A Valerius, member of a popular family, was appointed. He renewed the concessions made in the preceding year, and peace was, for the time, declared.

---

[*] A dictator's authority was superior to that of a regular magistrate; he was, in fact, absolute, though he was liable to be called to account for his actions. He could not hold office for more than six months.

But when the dictator, after a vain attempt to induce the Senate to make some permanent arrangement for the benefit of the debtors, resigned his office, the anger of the people became fiercer than ever. The army had not been disbanded, and the oath of obedience to the consul, as commander, was still binding. Some of the fiercer spirits would have found a way out of this difficulty by violence. "Slay the tyrant," they cried, "and we shall recover our freedom." Happily, their violent counsels did not find any favour with the majority.

The policy which they followed was one of "passive resistance." They marched, armed as they were, out of Rome, crossed the Anio, a river which flows into the Tiber, some seven miles above the city, and occupied an eminence which was afterwards called the Sacred Hill. They attacked no one; they threatened no one; but they said to the privileged classes—not in so many words, but by acts which were not less significant—"Give us our rights; do not take an unfair advantage of our needs—or fight your own battles; we will have nothing to do with a country in which life is not worth living."

To this argument the Senate had no answer. They could not use force—the movement was described as the "Secession of the People," and they could not do without them. All business was at a standstill, and, what was more serious, the city was defenceless. They had recourse to negotiation and compromise. They sent one of their number, Menenius Agrippa by name, a man highly esteemed for wisdom and the power of persuasive speech.

We are told that Agrippa put the argument which he had to address to his audience in the shape of a fable. "There was once," he said, "a dissension among the members of the human body. The working members, as the eyes, the hands, the feet, complained that they laboured for the benefit of the stomach, which remained idle, receiving the good things provided by the toil of others and doing nothing in return. They resolved to put an end to so unjust a state of things; they would work no more for this idler in the midst of them. But they found that this meant their own ruin. The idle stomach did work, in its turn: it assimilated what it received, and returned it to the members from which it came. If they starved it they were, in effect, starving themselves."

It is said that the people were so affected by this reasoning, that they returned to their homes and to their ordinary employments. Doubtless, some alteration of the debtors' condition took place. That the trouble was entirely removed must not be supposed. It remained, as it must remain as long as human nature continues to be the same, sometimes acute, sometimes dormant, according as times were bad or good.

The Law of the Twelve Tables, in which the frightful provision for the division of a debtor's body among his creditors is enacted, was later in date than the Secession. There can be no doubt, however, but that the plebeians made a great advance in their struggle for political equality. They secured the privilege of having magistrates of their own, the Tribunes of the People of whom we hear so much in Roman history.

They were to be regularly appointed champions and guardians of liberty.

The powers of the Tribunes were very large. They could call any magistrate to account; they could fine and even imprison a consul; they could stop any proceeding; they could call an assembly of the people; they could protect any citizen that appealed to them. In order that they might be able to do these things without fear of consequences, they were guarded against any attack. The person of a tribune was sacred. Anyone who ventured to kill or injure him fell under a curse.

On the other hand their powers were narrowly limited. They could not propose a law; their position for a long time was purely negative, and their action was often impeded by the provision that they had to be unanimous. In early days this does not seem to have been imposed.

As time went on their powers became more developed and this provision was enacted. At the same time their number was greatly increased. This gave their opponents an opportunity of which they availed themselves. When there were ten tribunes, it was easy to find one who could be persuaded, or, it may be, bribed to help the aristocratic party. Yet, after all, the tribuneship was one of the great bulwarks of Roman liberty. It was a substantial and permanent result of the "Bloodless Revolution."

CHAPTER IV

BACK TO THE LAND

SCARCELY less urgent than the question of the treatment of the debtor was that of the occupation and ownership of land. It was fiercely debated for hundreds of years.

The earliest attempt to settle it was made, it would seem, about twenty-four years after the expulsion of the Kings; it came up again and again while the Republic lasted; it remained still calling for settlement when the Republic gave place to the Empire.

Many laws dealing with it were passed, but all were more or less evaded. It would be too much to say that no good was done by them, but it is certainly true that the abuses which they were intended to remove, still remained, and in the end did much to bring about the ruin of the State.

The property in dispute was the land which belonged to the State *(ager publicus)*. This land had been acquired by conquest. The spread of Roman power was gradual, the neighbouring towns with their territories becoming subject to it on different terms.

There was no such wholesale change of owner-ship as took place in England when it passed into the hands of the Norman conquerors. Then, as we learn from the great survey known as the Domesday-book, practically the whole of the land of England, that only excepted which belonged to the Church, passed into the hands of William I., and was distributed among his kinsmen and followers.

In the case of Rome, on the contrary, part of the land was retained by the old proprietors, part was given back to them on terms, part was sold at once, but a large portion was reserved as public property.

It was this last portion that was the chief subject of dispute. The abuse complained of was that it was monopolised by persons whose birth or wealth made them persons of influence; the remedy proposed was that no one should occupy more than a certain amount, and that the surplus should be divided among those citizens who needed it. (It should be observed that in all cases the land was *occupied, not owned*, being rented for long periods, with a general custom of renewal when the lease came to an end.)

The greatest amount was fixed at 500 *iugera*,[*] about 310 acres.

Later on, a certain relaxation was granted. A man might hold the five hundred *iugera* in his own name, and half as much in the name of a son, but not more than one thousand were to be held by any one family. Another provision was to the effect that on

---

[*] A *iugerum* was equal to 2 roods 19 poles.

every holding a certain amount of free labour, in proportion to its size, should be employed.

It may be said that all the great social and economical questions with which the ancient world was troubled are still with us in one shape or another. This is certainly true of the land question. The small holding and the large domain still represent opposing interests. In Australia the squatter, occupying huge territories on which he keeps hundreds of thousands of sheep, looks jealously on new settlers. In Ireland the large grazing farms are at this very time an object of popular hostility.

Slave labour is happily banished from a large part of the world, but even of this something still survives. The white man complains that he is driven out of the field by the competition of inferior races, who are able to live on wages which mean for him something like starvation.

In Rome, as I have said, the matter was never settled. A curious illustration of the difficulties which faced the reformer is supplied. A certain Caius Licinius Stolo was one of the principal promoters of a proposal for restricting the amount of the *ager publicus* which might be held by any one man. The struggle lasted for ten years; the proposal then became law.

Before two years had passed, however, Licinius himself was fined for evading it. He held the maximum of land in his own name, and he contrived to get possession of as much more by taking it in the name of his son, whom, for this purpose, he made independent. (A father had by the Roman law something like absolute power over his children. This was known as the "father's authority," *patria potestas*. He could give this up, if he saw fit, and the son became independent, free, for instance, to hold property in his own name. Licinius released his son with a secret understanding that the profits of the property should come to himself.)

The punishment inflicted on Licinius did not put a stop to the practice. In this and in other ways the law was made ineffective. Two centuries afterwards the evil had grown to such a height that another agitation was commenced in the hope of doing away with it. The Licinian law was passed in 367 B.C. In 133 B.C. Tiberius Gracchus proposed the very same restriction, getting it passed into a law, having officers appointed to carry it out, and yet, it would seem, really accomplishing very little.

It is certain that as time went on Italy was more and more occupied by large domains, vast farmholdings worked by the labour of slaves. The Italian yeoman who had been the backbone of the Roman armies, the man who lived on "the ancestral farm with its modest home," had disappeared.

CHAPTER V

LIBERTY, EQUALITY, AND FRATERNITY

SO far we have seen how the Roman Commons struggled for liberty. The rich man was not to take advantage of the power which money put into his hands, was not to turn his poor neighbour into a slave; he was not to take to himself what by right belonged to all; the public land was not to be held by a few rich men; room was to be left for the humble homesteads of the poor.

These, it may be said, were demands for liberty. But this was soon seen not to be enough. As a matter of fact, a man cannot be really free unless he has a voice in the management of public affairs. If he is to live happily and contentedly under laws, he must have a share in the making of them. If they are framed for him by others, he is sure to find, or at the least to think, that they are oppressive and unfair. So he goes on to demand equality. When economic wrongs, injustices, that is, in the matter of property, had been set right, political grievances had to be redressed. After liberty had been secured, the next thing that was sought for was equality.

The Commons, as we have seen, had their Tribunes to defend them. The power of these magistrates was largely increased in the process of time, but for a while it was narrowly limited. They could prevent things from being done, but they could do little or nothing themselves. If the plebeians (*plebeii* and *patricii* were the two classes of the Roman people) were to have a real share in the management of public affairs, they must have the right of being elected as magistrates. First the plebeians had to obtain the right of intermarriage with the patricians. For a time these mixed marriages took place, but were attended by certain disabilities. Then they were legalised. Children born of them were put on exactly the same footing as their fellow-citizens. The plebeian in the year 445 obtained the *ius connubii* or "right of marriage." The important gain was that whereas before the children of a mixed marriage could not perform certain religious rites without which office could not be held, this disability was now removed. It will be observed that this was the first success, and in a way the most important of all. It cleared the way to equality.

The first magistracy that was thrown open to them was the Quæstorship, an office that was connected with the collecting and expending of the public money. This is what we should expect. Men who had to earn their own livelihood would have business habits which would make them useful in money matters.

The Quæstorship was only one step, and, except as a beginning, not a very important one; the great aim of the plebeian was the Consulship. This was not so easily gained. The first plebeian quæstor was appointed in 421 B.C. It was not till more than half a century later that the battle for the Consulship was won. And even then the victory was not complete. Year after year, under one pretence or another, the patricians contrived to make the election of a plebeian consul void. They discovered something irregular about it—the religious authorities were the judges in such matters, and these were still taken from the old families.

It was not till 342 B.C. that the rule was permanently established. After that date one of the Consulships was always reserved for a plebeian. In course of time the distinction between the two orders was almost forgotten. Old families died out; new ones acquired wealth and honour, dwelt in palaces as splendid as any that the old nobles possessed, and could show on occasion the busts of statesmen and soldiers as distinguished as any that figured in the oldest pedigrees.

During all this time there had been going on a great social change. The two Orders had been for a time kept as separate as two hostile nations which happened to dwell in close neighbourhood might have been. This was easy enough as long as the distinction between them was real, as long as a patrician was richer, better educated, better mannered than his plebeian neighbour. Even then personal feelings sometimes were stronger than their class barriers.

When these outward differences ceased to exist, and a plebeian could not be distinguished in look or manner or mode of life from a patrician, then the class separation ceased to exist. A few families probably kept up, more or less, the old exclusiveness; most of them dropped it.

The narrative is illustrated by one of those picturesque anecdotes which are so often attached to the history of a great movement. It would be a mistake to look in such incidents for the causes of important changes; that they are often the occasion cannot be doubted. Livy gives it under date of the year 374, when the plebeians had gained the legal right to office, but were often in practice excluded. The historian attributes this exclusion not to the pride of the patricians, but to the depressed condition of the plebeians, and then proceeds to tell his readers how a remedy was found.

"M. Fabius Ambustus was a man of weight in his own order and also among the Commons, because they did not regard him as one inclined to look down upon them. The elder of his two daughters was married to Servius Sulpicius, the younger to C. Licinius Stolo, a man of distinction, but a plebeian. The latter alliance had won for Fabius much popularity among the Commons. It so happened that the two sisters were amusing themselves with conversation in the house of Sulpicius, who was then a Tribune with consular power. Sulpicius coming home from the Forum, one of his lictors, according to custom, knocked at the door with his rod. The younger Fabia, not knowing what it meant, was frightened; her sister, surprised at her ignorance, could not help laughing. The laugh left a sting, for a woman is often touched by a trifle. At the same time, the crowd of attendants, and of people offering their services, made her envy her sister's position and repine at her own—there are few who are content to see their equals preferred to themselves. Her father saw her while the wound was yet fresh, and asked her whether all was well. She would have concealed the cause of her trouble; it seemed hardly kind to her sister or respectful to her husband. The father's affectionate inquiries, however, brought out the cause: she was unhappy because she had married into a house which no dignities or honours could enter. He consoled her with the assurance that she should shortly see in her own house the same honours which she had seen at her sister's."

CHAPTER VI

A GREAT DISASTER

IT was well that the Roman State made some advance towards unity and harmony in the hundred and twenty years that followed the expulsion of the kings, for in 390 B.C. it suffered a blow which might well have been fatal. A large part of Northern Italy had for some years been in the hands of invading tribes which, from time to time, had made their way by passes of the Alps from Gaul into Italy. Rome had doubtless received some benefit from these movements. The Etrurian cities had been more or less occupied with defending themselves against their enemies on the north, and had been content to leave their neighbours on the south alone.

In 391 B.C. a tribe of Italian Gauls, finding their territories too narrow for them, and possibly pressed by newcomers from the north, invaded Etruria, and attacked the city of Clusium. The people of Clusium sent envoys to Rome, asking for help.

The Romans did not think fit to send troops—it would have been a serious matter to levy an army for what may be called foreign service—but sent an embassy which was to represent to the Gauls that Clusium was a friendly city and must be left alone. The Gauls replied: "We have no wish to injure Clusium, but it has more land than it needs, while we have not enough. Let it give us a share, and we shall be content. If it refuses, stand by, and see whether we cannot make good our claims by force of arms."

The Roman ambassadors, three haughty young nobles—so the story runs—asked: "What are Gauls doing in Etruria? By what right do you come?" "By the right of our swords," was the answer. A battle followed, and the Roman ambassadors had the imprudence to take part in it. One of them struck down a Gallic chief, and was recognised as he stripped the fallen man of his arms. The Gauls at once drew off from the field. It was with Rome, not with Clusium, that they had thenceforward to deal.

They sent envoys demanding the surrender of the three men who had so grossly offended against the law of nations. The Senate asked counsel of the Priestly College which had to do with such matters. The college replied that the offenders ought to be given up. But the Senate hesitated. The three men belonged to what was then the most powerful family in Rome, the great Fabian House. Whether they referred the matter to the decision of the whole body of the people is not clear. In any case the people expressed its opinion in a way that could not be mistaken, for they elected the three envoys among the Military Tribunes for the next year. [*]

---

[*] The office of Consul was at the time in abeyance. It was put, so to speak, into commission, and was executed by six *Tribuni Militares*.

The election took place, it is probable, late in the year. For this reason, and also, it is probable, because they thought it well to wait for reinforcements from kinsmen beyond the Alps, the Gauls did not immediately act on the challenge thus thrown down. It was not till the summer of the following year that they marched on Rome. They attacked no one on their way; their one thought seemed to be to avenge the insult which had been offered to them.

The Romans, on the other hand, were strangely insensible to their danger. They raised an army, indeed, partly of home levies, partly of allies, but no special care was taken to make it equal to the occasion; even in point of numbers it was insufficient. It was remembered afterwards that the religious ceremony with which it was usual to begin a campaign was omitted.

The army took up its position at a place about eleven miles from the city, where a small brook named the Allia fell into the Tiber. The battle that followed was soon over. The Gallic king, Brennus *(Bran)* by name, charged the Roman line at the point where probably an attack was least expected, the rising ground occupied by the right wing.

The fury of the Gallic warriors carried all before them, much as some twenty centuries later Prince Charlie's Highlanders did at Prestonpans. Then they turned their victorious arms on the centre, which had been weakened to prolong the line, and on the left. There, too, the victory was rapid and complete.

The Romans fled precipitately across the river. Some were drowned; not a few were crushed to death by their comrades. The survivors made their way with headlong speed to Rome. The rout of Allia was rightly held to be one of the most disgraceful incidents in the Roman annals, and the day on which it happened (July 18th) was marked in the calendar as one of those on which no business could be transacted.

For two days the conquerors remained on the field of battle, celebrating their victory with revel, or, as the historian suggests, fearing that the speedy flight of the enemy concealed some deep design. On the third day they marched to Rome. They found the city deserted, with the exception of the Capitol, which was occupied by a garrison of picked men.

In the Forum, however, a strange spectacle met their eyes. There, seated on chairs of state, sat a company of venerable citizens. They were too old to be of any service in defending the Capitol; to fly from Rome seemed unworthy of their rank. Perhaps they might serve their country in the only way that was possible to them, by a death that would expiate its sin. The Gauls gazed on them with respectful astonishment. At last a barbarian ventured to stroke the beard of one of them. The old man, wroth at the familiarity, smote the man with his ivory staff. The Gaul, resenting the insult of a blow, slew him, and all the others met with the same fate.

Though the city was in the hands of the barbarians, Rome was not wholly lost. The Capitol was held by a strong garrison, too numerous, it may well be, for the room which it offered and for the store of provisions which it could hold: a large force had been col-

"The old man, wroth at the familiarity,
smote the man with his ivory staff."

lected at Veii, made up of fugitives from Allia, eager to wipe out their disgrace, and others who were longing for an opportunity to serve their country.

The invaders, on the other hand, were beginning to suffer in various ways. Rome, never a very healthy place, was particularly dangerous during the heat of summer. It was deserted at this season by all who could contrive to get away, and these strangers from a more temperate climate naturally suffered more than natives. Supplies began to run short. The stores found in the houses had been wastefully used; much had perished in the fires which broke out in the deserted city. The Gauls soon found themselves compelled to plunder the neighbouring country, and suffered much at the hands of enemies who were familiar with every spot, and were always on the watch to cut off stragglers.

Once indeed they were very near to a great success, nothing less than the capture of the Capitol itself. A messenger, despatched by the garrison to their countrymen at Veii, had contrived to make the expedition unobserved, but had left some trace of his movements. This the Gauls had not failed to detect, and they conceived the idea of a surprise.

The Romans had a very narrow escape. The sentinels were asleep; no such attacks had been made before; even the dogs were silent. So the Gauls were able to climb unobserved almost to the summit of the hill; but the geese which were penned in the temple of Juno heard their approach and began to cackle. The birds were sacred to the goddess, and though provisions had by this time run very short, they had not been touched, and their provender had been spared from the scanty rations of the men. This piety was now to be rewarded.

The clamorous birds roused a certain Marius Manlius from his slumbers; he hastily armed himself and ran to the edge of the cliff, just in time to hurl down the foremost of the attacking party. The enterprise, which could only have succeeded as a surprise, was abandoned, and the Capitol was saved. The incident was one of the most famous in Roman story. Virgil, in his description of the shield on which Vulcan pictured for Æneas the coming fortunes of his race, thus described it:—

"There Manlius on Tarpeian steep
Stood firm, the Capitol to keep.
A silver goose in gilded walls
With flapping wings announced the Gauls;
And through the wood the invaders crept,
And climbed the height while others slept.
Golden their hair on head and chin:
Gold collars deck their milk-white skin:
　　Short cloaks with colour checked
Shine on their backs: two spears each wields
Of Alpine make: and oblong shields
　　Their brawny limbs protect."
　　　　Æn. VIII. (Conington's Translation).

"Just in time to hurl down the foremost of
the attacking party."

Both sides were now growing weary of the conflict. The Gauls, suffering grievously from sickness and from scarcity, were longing to return to their native land; with the garrison things had come to an almost desperate pass. It was agreed that a large sum should be paid in gold, and that the invaders should depart. The agreement was carried out, and Rome was once more free.

Brennus and the gold.

Two picturesque stories, which are told of the last scene, may be repeated as they stand, without too precise an inquiry into their truth. According to one,

42

when the gold was being weighed, Brennus, the Gallic king, threw his sword—the Gallic swords were notably long and heavy—into the scale in which lay the weights. When the Roman commissioners remonstrated, he cried out "Woe to the conquered!" *(Væ victis)*, and the Romans had to submit.

The other saved the Roman pride by representing that, just at the critical moment, Camillus, who had been duly appointed Dictator by the magistrates who were serving in the garrison of the Capitol, came up and drove the overbearing conquerors in headlong rout from the city. Rome had suffered the disgrace of having to bargain for her freedom, but not the crowning shame of having actually to buy off her conquerors.

The Gauls continued to be formidable enemies. From time to time during the next two centuries they appeared, carrying a sudden terror over the prosperous fields of Northern Italy—the Romans had a special word, indicative of sudden confusion and uproar *(tumultus)*, to express their onslaughts—but they never again brought the great city so near to the brink of ruin.

CHAPTER VII

FORMIDABLE NEIGHBOURS

OF all the enemies whom Rome had to encounter as she widened her borders, especially in her expansions eastward and southward, the strongest and most obstinate were the Samnites. Of one tribe belonging to this great stock, the Sabines, we have already heard. But the Sabines were incorporated with Rome in quite early days; their more distant kinsmen remained independent far down into the third century of Roman history.

For a while it might have seemed an open question which of the two powers would be supreme in the Italian peninsula. The Samnites were not unworthy of the place. They had some, at least, of the virtues which fit a nation for empire: they were brave, frugal, of simple life, and blameless manners. The Roman poets were never wearied of holding up to their countrymen the virtues of the Samnite peasant and his frugal wife as examples to be imitated. And for a time it seemed as if this valiant and vigorous race would hold, and more than hold, its own.

Towards the end of the fifth century B.C. they had descended from their hills and conquered the fertile plains of Campania. Thus they possessed them-

44

selves of a territory which stretched nearly across Italy. They never, strictly speaking, touched the Adriatic or Upper Sea, but they held the shores of the Tyrrhenian or Lower from the borders of Latium almost down to the southern extremity of the peninsula. The quality in which they seemed to have been deficient was the power of holding together. In great emergencies they would appoint a commander-in-chief, under whom all the tribes were, more or less, willing to act; but, for the most part, the different sections of the race preferred to hold aloof from each other.

We know, it is true, but little of Samnite history. What has come down to us we learn from the Roman historians. Still, this fact of the strong local feeling with its discriminating effect seems to come out.

It is peculiarly interesting to us in these days, because race feeling has again become a very powerful element in politics. The causes are, indeed, entirely different. Influences of which these Samnite tribesmen, a wholly uncultured people, with no history and no literature, knew nothing, are developing the same passion of separation. It is the people which can look back to a history of its own, and possesses a language and a literature of which it is reasonably proud, that resents the union in which its own nationality seems to be lost. It is impossible not to feel some sympathy with the sentiment, but it does not tend to the making of a strong and stable State.

It is impossible to tell in detail the story of the long struggle between Rome and Samnium. It lasted for more than half a century, the first Samnite war

beginning in 343 B.C., the third being brought to a con-
clusion in 290 B.C. This does not mean, it is true, that
the Samnites were never afterwards seen in arms
against Rome, but they never again played the part of a
principal antagonist.

Still, warriors of the race long continued to seize
every opportunity of measuring swords with their old
enemy, and thus, in the armies of Pyrrhus and of Hannibal they never failed to keep up its old reputation for
valour. In the Social War, the last struggle against
Rome, in which the Italian tribes sought to destroy the
union which was called alliance, but was felt to be
bondage, it was in the ancient Samnium that the rebellion found its most sturdy supporters.

The first Samnite war lasted two years only, but
it brought a great accession of power to Rome, for it
made her the dominant power in the rich plains and
wealthy cities of Campania. It was brought to an end,
too, most opportunely, for a new difficulty was about
to present itself. The Latins said in effect to Rome,
"Let us go our own way, or give us full rights of citizenship with you." Neither demand could be granted,
and the question had to be settled on the battlefield.

Of this Latin war two stories are told which
illustrate the spirit in which the Romans did their duty
as soldiers. The first shows the unbending severity of
their discipline. The two armies were confronting each
other, when a noble youth from the Latin town of
Tusculum rode into the space between the two and
challenged any one of the warriors of Rome to single
combat. Manlius Torquatus, the Consul in command,

had strictly forbidden the acceptance of any such challenge, but his son, provoked beyond endurance by the
taunts of the Latin champion, rode out from the ranks,
engaged and vanquished his antagonist, and then
returning to his own line laid the spoils at his father's
feet. The stern old man made no reply save to declare
that his son had incurred the penalty of death by his
disobedience, and the sentence was actually carried
out.

The other incident is the self-sacrifice of Decius
Mus at the battle of Veseris in 340 B.C. He devoted
himself to the Gods of the Dead, set spur to his horse,
and rode into the lines of the enemy, where he perished. Armies led by such men, ready as they were to
surrender life, and what was dearer than life, to serve
their country, could hardly fail to conquer.

In 338 B.C. the Latin war came to an end, and
the Latin cities became one with the Roman State. But
all were not received on the same terms. Some obtained full citizenship; to others citizenship without
political power was given. A few were severely punished by confiscation and the banishment of their chief
citizens. The Roman policy was wanting in far-
sightedness, and trouble came, as it was bound to
come, in after years from this cause.

Three years after the battle of Veseris the second Samnite war began, and lasted with one interval,
when truce was made for a year, from 327 down to
304 B.C. At one time it seemed possible that Rome
might lose what she had been painfully acquiring for
more than two hundred years.

In 321 B.C. her army suffered a disaster which ranked with the rout of Allia and with the frightful slaughter of Cannæ, of which I shall have to speak hereafter. The Roman army had entered the Samnite territory, and was awaiting the movements of the enemy. Intelligence reached the consuls that the principal town in the friendly region of Lucania was threatened by the Samnite forces. They immediately broke up their camp and marched southwards.

The shortest way lay through a narrow valley, known as the Forks, or, as we should say, the Gorge of Caudium. Not dreaming of danger, for they believed the enemy to be many miles to the southward, the army entered the valley, without any precaution being taken. When they reached the further end they found the passage barred. They hastily retraced their steps, to find the entrance similarly secured. The intelligence had been false. The Samnite army was present in full force, and the Romans were caught in a trap from which they could not possibly get free.

The Samnite general, Caius Pontius, did not know what to do with the splendid booty which he had captured. He sent to ask the advice of his father. The old man was brought to the camp in a wagon. His counsel was to this effect: "You must either let them go without conditions, or you must destroy them all. By the first course you will win the friendship of Rome; by the second you will cripple her power so effectually that for a generation at least Samnium will be able to remain in peace."

Caius Pontius was not prepared to adopt either plan. He chose a middle course which was neither generous nor safe. He made the consuls and the chief officers of the legions swear to a treaty of which the terms were that the Romans should retire from the territory of Samnium, that they should give up two colonies* which protected Latium, and that Rome should recognise the ancient alliance between the two nations. These provisions put an effectual bar to all schemes of Roman expansion. The army was allowed to depart unharmed, but every man had to pass under the yoke (two spears crossed), without arms and wearing each a single garment.

The Public Assembly at Rome refused to accept a treaty so ruinous and so humiliating. Had Pontius expected any other result he must have been very much wanting in sagacity. His proper course was to keep the army in his power till the treaty was ratified. As it was, he had no hold upon anyone but the generals and officers who had taken the oath. These were surrendered to him. He refused to accept them, demanding that the whole treaty should be considered void, and that the Roman army should be replaced in the position from which he had released them. This was, of course, refused, and the Samnites reaped practically no advantage from the affair.

It is not easy to say which of the two parties has the best claim to our sympathy. On the one hand the conduct of Rome was not honourable. She could not

---

* A colony was a military post. A town or village was occupied by discharged soldiers, each of whom had his allotment of land.

get quit of a heavy obligation by a surrender which cost her so little. On the other hand the Samnite commander could not fairly ask that the army should be put back in its place of imprisonment. The disgrace to which he had subjected it would have to count for something. It was the price which it had had to pay for liberty, and it was a price which could not be repaid.

The struggle between the two nations was as fierce as it was long, but it ended in the complete victory of Rome. One of the last Samnite victims was the Pontius who had won, or, we may say, lost at Caudium. He was taken prisoner in a campaign almost thirty years after the affair of the "Caudine Forks," carried to Rome, compelled to walk in the triumphal procession behind the Consul's chariot, and then put to death. It was an ungenerous act, but it serves to show that the disgrace had not been forgotten.

CHAPTER VIII

A MASTER OF STRATEGY

ALL the experience that had been gained, all the forti-
tude that had been acquired by the Romans in their
long struggles with the Etrurian and Latin Leagues,
and with Samnium, were needed to carry them safely
through the war in which they were next engaged.

The southern part of the Italian peninsula was
occupied by a number of Greek cities. The most flour-
ishing age of these cities seems to have been at the
time of the Roman kings. The next century saw them
beginning to decay. Some of the States were hard
pressed by the Italian tribes. When Rome began to extend her influence in this direction some of the cities
had fallen into Italian hands and all were more or less
weakened.

There is no need, however, to dwell on the early
relations between Rome and these communities. I may
pass on at once to the story of how she came into collision with Tarentum, which had by this time become
the most powerful among them. In 303 B.C. a treaty
was concluded between the two cities, one of the conditions being that no Roman ship should pass the
promontory of Iapyx (Cape Leuca). This provision was

violated in 282 B.C. by the appearance of a Roman squadron in the Gulf of Tarentum and even in the harbour of the city. The Tarentines attacked it and sank five out of the ten ships and captured another. The Roman admiral fell in the battle. An embassy sent to lodge a complaint was greatly insulted in the Public Assembly, and Rome had nothing left but to declare war. She had her hands full for the moment and tried to settle the question peaceably. For a time it seemed likely that a peaceful policy would prevail.

There was a strong pro-Roman party in Tarentum. Some of her citizens had intelligence enough to see that the true policy of the State was to make friends with the city which had already become the leading power in Italy. They carried the people with them, and one of their leaders was made Dictator.

Before anything was settled there came news that changed the whole aspect of affairs. The most famous soldier of the day, Pyrrhus, King of Epirus, offered to help Tarentum. The peace proposals were promptly abandoned; the Roman army, which was not strong enough to take any decisive action, retired northward. Winter was spent on both sides in active preparation for a campaign.

The Roman general Lævinus was the first in the field. It was of the greatest importance to prevent the disaffected tribesmen of Southern Italy from joining the Greek king. Lævinus proceeded south by forced marches, and reached the Siris, a river which flows into the sea about twenty miles west of Tarentum before Pyrrhus had time to complete his plans.

The king's position was one of great difficulty. He had not been joined by the Italian allies on whose help he had counted. The troops that he had brought with him were all that he could wish, but the levies which he had raised in Tarentum were of inferior quality. He offered himself to the Romans as an arbitrator. They replied by asking him what business he had in Italy. He saw that he must fight; to delay would be to lose all his prestige and with it all hope of Italian help. He marched to the Siris and encamped on the left or eastern bank. The Roman entrenchments were in full sight and impressed him by their appearance. "The order of these Barbarians"—the Greeks then and for a long time afterwards spoke of the Romans as Barbarians—"is far from barbarous." Lævinus, whose interest it was to fight at once, forced a passage of the river, and engaged the enemy at close quarters.

The struggle was long and fierce. At one time it was reported that Pyrrhus had fallen—a near kinsman of the king had been slain—and the king had to ride along the line bareheaded to assure his troops. At last a force which the Romans had never before seen in the field was launched against them. Pyrrhus had brought with him twenty elephants, and these huge animals, each with a miniature castle on its back, struck terror into the hostile lines, and made the horses absolutely unmanageable.

The Romans were driven across the Siris, but managed to maintain their order, nor was Pyrrhus strong enough to interfere with their retreat. Both sides lost heavily. To one who congratulated him on his success, Pyrrhus replied, "One more such victory will ruin me." A "Pyrrhic victory" has passed into a proverb to denote a gain which can scarcely be distinguished from a loss.

But the actual number of the slain and wounded did not represent the whole result of the victory. It set fire, so to speak, to a smouldering mass of discontent. The Samnites, whose memories of independence were still fresh, joined Pyrrhus in great numbers; yet there was no general rising against Rome. He marched northward and came within twenty miles of the city.

He had already attempted persuasion, sending his confidential minister, Cineas by name, to Rome, with the terms on which he would be willing to make peace. Briefly, these were that Rome must give up all claims to Southern Italy, restoring her conquests on the Italian Tiber and promising to leave the Greek cities alone. There were some, it was said, who were willing to make peace on such conditions.

The general feeling was strongly adverse, and was vigorously expressed by the most venerable of Roman statesmen. Appius Claudius, surnamed "the blind," rose in the Senate and said: "Never before have I rejoiced in my blindness, and I would willingly be deaf that I might not hear proposals which are fatal to the dignity of Rome. We have flattered ourselves that if the great Alexander had come hither, he would have come hither in vain. Who is this Pyrrhus? He comes to Italy because there is no place for him in Greece."

The old man carried the Senate with him; Cineas was sent back to Pyrrhus with this answer: "If you would have Rome for your friend, you must leave

Italy." The king then advanced, but he did not find the support on which he counted. The Latins, the Etrurians, and other neighbours of Rome, were not willing to exchange her sway for that of Greece. So King Pyrrhus retired to Tarentum.

The next move was made by Rome. The Senate sent envoys to the king. They came, they said, to bargain for an exchange of prisoners. Pyrrhus believed that they had other objects. He tried to win them by bribery, a method in which Macedonian statesmen had great faith, and not without reason. The gold was refused with contempt. Then he tried terror.

In the midst of an interview with Fabricius, the principal envoy, a curtain was withdrawn and an elephant stretched out his trunk over the Roman's head and loudly trumpeted. "Neither your gold nor your beasts move me," was the answer of Fabricius. In the matter of the prisoners Pyrrhus behaved with much generosity. One account is that he released them without making any conditions; another and more likely account states that he let them return for a while on parole.

But the war went on. A battle was fought at Asculum in 297 B.C. and ended much as that already described, in a nominal victory. This time, however, Pyrrhus was wounded, and as everything depended on this one great man it was a serious loss.

The next year nothing was done, but Fabricius had an opportunity of making a return for the generosity of the king which has been already mentioned. One of the royal servants offered to murder his master.

"An elephant stretched out his trunk over
the Roman's head and loudly trumpeted."

Fabricius at once informed Pyrrhus of the matter. Negotiations were again attempted, but Rome had no other terms to offer than that Pyrrhus must leave Italy. Leave it he did, sailing to Sicily, where he hoped to establish himself, so as to be able to renew the struggle with Rome. In Sicily he gained no permanent success, and in 276 B.C. he returned to Italy. But he effected nothing.

The veterans whom he had brought with him five years before had nearly disappeared, and with all his generalship, and this with common consent was unequalled in his day,[1] he could not make untrained Italians into an effective force. At Maleventum[2] he suffered a crushing defeat, retreating with a few horsemen to Tarentum. Not long afterwards he crossed into Greece and there perished two years later, again fighting in a quarrel which was not his own. It was at Argos, and in a faction fight, that he perished, by much the same fate that overtook Abimelech, the son of Gideon. A woman felled him to the ground with a tile which she hurled from a house-top, and a soldier despatched him as he lay insensible.

Pyrrhus was a soldier of a type for which the Romans had no kind of admiration. Destined themselves to conquer the civilised world by force of arms, they had nothing of the temper of the military adventurer. His purposeless ambition was a stock subject for their moralists. Plutarch has preserved one of these

---

[1] Hannibal is said to have thought him inferior only to the great Alexander.

[2] A name afterwards changed to Beneventum—"Illcome to Welcome."

themes in which the king's prime minister, Cineas, is the champion of reason.

"Sire," said this philosophic statesman, when the preparations for the invasion of Italy were occupying the king's attention, "these Romans have the reputation of being excellent soldiers, and have the command of many warlike tribes; if by favour of the gods we conquer them, what use shall we make of our victory?"

"Your question," said the king, "answers itself. Rome once subdued, there is no town, Greek or barbarian, in the whole peninsula that will venture to oppose us. We shall, in fact, be masters of Italy, and what that means no one knows better than you."

"And what, Sire, shall we do next when Italy has been conquered?"

"Sicily is at hand, and stretches out her hands to receive us—a fertile and populous island, but torn by internal dissensions, and easily to be conquered," answered Pyrrhus.

"Nothing seems more reasonable, my prince," Cineas continued: "and is the conquest of Sicily to conclude our undertakings?"

"Heaven forbid!" cried Pyrrhus. "Africa and Carthage are within reach. We have seen how narrowly they escaped subjugation by a man who was actually a fugitive from his own city of Syracuse, and had nothing but a small squadron of ships.* When we have accomplished this, who will venture to resist?"

* Agathocles, tyrant of Syracuse, 318-289 B.C.

58

"No one, certainly," replied Cineas. "You will recover Macedonia, and make yourself master of all Greece. And then?"

"Then we will take our ease, and eat and drink and be merry," cried the king.

"But, Sire, why should we not do so now?" said the philosopher. "We have all that we want ready to our hand. In fact, we are already in possession of what you propose to reach through seas of blood, and after infinite troubles brought upon others and suffered by ourselves."

The Romans after a long and desperate struggle had vanquished the most formidable foe that had ever come against them. Their courage, their tenacity of purpose, the true soldierly qualities which made the most defective institutions somehow serve their purpose, had their reward. The final defeat of Pyrrhus left no formidable rival in the field. Tarentum was taken in 272 B.C., and in the course of the next seven or eight years Rome had established an undisputed sway in the whole Italian Peninsula, Cisalpine Gaul alone excepted.

CHAPTER IX

THE BEGINNINGS OF EMPIRE

WE must not suppose that when the Romans had made themselves undisputed masters of Italy they began to think of conquering other lands. This is not the way in which empires begin. This or that citizen may have had ambitious schemes, but, probably, the nation as a whole would have been content to stay within the boundaries which seemed to have been so conveniently arranged.

Circumstances were, however, too strong for it. There came a call which it seemed unwise to refuse. So were taken the first steps of a movement which was to extend over the whole of Western Europe, Northern Africa, and Western Asia as far as the Euphrates; and this call came from very near, from a land which might almost be said to be a part of Italy, from the island of Sicily.

Something must be said of the power with which Rome thus came into collision. Carthage was a Phœnician city, the last of the colonies founded on the shores of the Mediterranean by Tyre. The date of the foundation is doubtful. The beginning of the city was probably in the same century as that of Rome. At the time of which I am now writing the Carthaginian power had spread over much of the Western Mediterranean. She was mistress of all the Phœnician colonies in Northern Africa and ruled the native tribes for some distance inland, she owned the islands of Corsica, Sardinia and Malta, and had gradually extended her sway over three-fourths of Sicily. It is with this part of her Empire that we are now concerned.

The eastern portion of Sicily was still possessed by Greek cities. At the time of which I am writing Syracuse was the only one out of the whole number which was of importance. Most of the other cities had fallen into the hands of Carthage, which, after more than two centuries of conflict, now seemed likely to acquire the whole island.

On the Sicilian side of the strait which divides Sicily from the mainland stood the town of Messana. In 289 B.C. it had been treacherously seized by some mercenary troops who had been in the pay of Agathocles, tyrant of Syracuse, and had been thrown out of employment by his death. They lived mainly by plunder, raiding the country and levying toll on the traffic that passed through the strait. For a time this business flourished, but when Syracuse fell into the vigorous hands of Hiero, the freebooters, who called themselves Mamertines, from *Mamers*, one of the forms of the word Mars,* found themselves in difficulties.

Accordingly they began to look about for help. One party looked to Rome, another to Carthage, and

* These Mamertines were Italians, having been originally enlisted in Campania.

each sent envoys to put their request before the power which they invoked. Carthage, or rather the Carthaginians, had the advantage of being close at hand. One of their generals, Hanno by name, was in command of a force in the neighbourhood. He marched to Messana at once, came to terms with the Syracusans who were besieging the town, and occupied the citadel. The news reached Rome, where the envoys were pleading their cause before the Senate.

That body was not a little perplexed. It saw that Rome was not called upon to meddle with the internal quarrels of a Greek city, and it knew that it was no light matter to provoke the hostility of so great a power as Carthage. It handed the matter over to the decision of the people, and the people, knowing little of the facts of the case, and naturally jealous of seeing Carthage firmly established within so small a distance from Italy, determined to send help to the Mamertines.

This business was very soon concluded. The Carthaginians had not made themselves liked in the town, and when the Roman admiral, a member of the great Claudian family, arrived there, he was heartily welcomed. A conference was arranged at which the leader of the Mamertines, Hanno, and Claudius were to be present. Hanno was arrested; the garrison in the citadel agreed to leave it, and together with their commander was permitted to depart.

When he reached home Hanno was put to death for having brought about the fall of Messana. Though war had not been formally proclaimed, it had practically commenced. It lasted altogether for about twenty-three years and was succeeded by a peace of about equal duration. The struggle was renewed in 219 B.C. and came to an end in 202 B.C. For nearly half a century after this Carthage was permitted to exist, but only because political factions at Rome could not agree as to what should be done with her.

Of one of the three parties concerned in the Sicilian quarrel little need be said. The Greek cities in the Island had shown the want of unity which was characteristic of the race, and had fallen one by one.

To Syracuse, in which at the last all that remained of Greek strength and energy was centred, another great vice of the Greek character, the fury of party spirit, proved fatal. For a time it was saved by the energy and prudence of its King, Hiero II. Hiero began with the very natural error of thinking that Carthage had the better chances of success. He soon found reasons for changing his opinion, and concluded an alliance with Rome. To this alliance he remained faithful for nearly half a century.

Of Carthage something has been already said. To all appearance she was much more powerful than her antagonist. A greater command of material strength she certainly had. A wide dominion, large and well-manned fleets, and a highly disciplined army was hers. In public spirit, in the higher kind of patriotism, she was deficient. She found her chief aim in the accumulation of wealth; she fought her battles with mercenaries. Gauls, Spaniards, Moors served in her army.

It was seldom that a native Carthaginian was found among the troops, except, indeed, in the higher ranks. Here they showed much military skill. One of the Carthaginian generals, the famous Hannibal, stands in the first rank of the great soldiers of history. Had he and others who were not far inferior to him been adequately supported by their countrymen, the issue of the conflict might well have been different from what it was.

I shall not attempt to tell in any detail the story of a war that lasted for nearly a quarter of a century. It will be sufficient to select some important and characteristic events.

The first is a story of how Rome became a naval power. Ships of war she had possessed for some time. An early treaty with Carthage, supposed to date from the end of the kingly or the beginning of the republican period had defined a limit beyond which a Roman fleet should not pass. There had been, as we have seen, a similar compact with Tarentum and no small trouble had followed the action of the Roman squadron which violated it. But there are ships and ships. At the present day there are junks in the Far East and the powerful battleships and the thirty-knot cruisers of Europe.

The Roman vessels, we may be sure, were rude in form and feeble in armament. The Carthaginians on the other hand had invented a highly developed art of construction and equipment from their Phœnician ancestors. In point of seamanship there could be no comparison between the two nations. One of them gained her knowledge of naval matters from coasting voyages only. The other was familiar with the Mediterranean from the coast of Palestine to the Straits of Gibraltar.

The Romans were soon convinced that they must do their best to correct this inequality. As long as Carthage commanded the sea, no real progress could be made. They could neither acquire the coast towns of Sicily, nor protect those of their own country. But the difficulty which they had to face was enormously great. They had to build ships which could meet the Carthaginian fleets on equal terms, and they had to raise a great force of seamen, with which to man them.

In the first matter a lucky accident helped them. It so happened that a Carthaginian "first-rate,"[*] as we should call it, was stranded somewhere on the coast of Southern Italy. It was taken as a model, and a number of vessels of a similar pattern were constructed. It was a bold undertaking, and a further illustration of Roman courage and tenacity of purpose, and it met with a success that could hardly have been expected. The manning of the new fleet was, in some respects, we may suppose, less difficult. A country with so long a coast line as Italy must necessarily have a considerable seafaring population, and from this a sufficient number of men could be impressed or induced to serve by good pay. That the new service was found to be very costly we know.

The first operation by sea was disastrous. One of the consuls sailed in advance of the main fleet with a squadron of seventeen vessels. On reaching Messana, he was advised to take possession of the island of

---

[*] A quinquereme—*i.e.*, a ship with five banks of oars.

Lipara, the chief of a volcanic group, near the north coast of Sicily. There he was surprised by the Carthaginian admiral, lost all his ships, and was himself taken prisoner.

The next incident in the campaign was of a very different character. The Carthaginians with fifty ships sailed northward to intercept the Roman fleet, fell in with it unexpectedly, and met with a complete defeat. It is very probable that they despised their enemy, neglected the usual precautions, and suffered accordingly.

It is likely that the same cause at least helped to produce the strange catastrophe that followed. It occurred to some ingenious person among the Romans that a combatant to whom the sea was unfamiliar would do well to make the conditions of a naval battle as similar as possible to those of a battle on land. Whether this person was Duilius or no we cannot say—he seems not to have joined the fleet till the idea had been carried out—but he gained the credit of it.

The Romans themselves did not feel able to manœuvre their ships like the enemy, but they could fight hand to hand better, they believed, than anyone else. If they were not skilful sailors who could accommodate themselves to changes of wind and weather, and use oar and rudder to the best advantage, yet, once put on the enemy's deck, they would more than hold their own.

To be able then to board an adversary's ship was what they aimed at. Each vessel was furnished with a boarding-bridge—they called it a "crow" (*cor*

"To be able to board an adversary's
ship was what they aimed at."

STORIES FROM ANCIENT ROME

vus), from the iron hook or grappling iron, which was not unlike a crow's beak. A pole was set up in its prow; to this a long ladder, broad enough for two men to pass abreast upon it, was attached in such a way that by means of a rope and pivot it could be swung round to any place where it could be used.

The Carthaginian admiral did his best, so to speak, to give effect to the Roman device. He made no attempt to manœuvre, but dashed straight at the hostile line of ships. Then the "crows" were brought into play. Ship after ship was grappled, boarded, and captured. The admiral himself had to abandon his galley, a splendid vessel which had once belonged to King Pyrrhus. As many as thirty Carthaginian ships were taken, and when the action was renewed a little later in the day, the number of captures was increased to fifty.

Mylæ—this place is a city on the northern coast of Sicily—gave its name to what is certainly one of the most decisive sea-fights in history. Duilius was covered with distinctions by his grateful countrymen. The honour of a triumph, the first naval triumph, was accorded to him. Two columns, appropriately adorned with beaks of ships, were erected in his honour, and he enjoyed, for the rest of his life, the privilege of being attended when he returned to his home from an entertainment by a musician and a torch-bearer. It sounds strange in modern ears, but we must remember that the Romans looked with much jealousy on all that seemed to give social distinction to an individual citizen.

One immediate result of the victory of Mylæ was that the island of Corsica was taken, or, at least, whatever power Carthage had possessed over that island was at an end. Probably this power did not extend far beyond the sea-coast. The city of Aleria was certainly taken by the Consul Scipio, and the exploit was considered to be of sufficient importance to be mentioned in his epitaph. The tribes of the interior probably paid as little regard to their new masters as they had done to their old.

Four years after Mylæ, another great battle was fought at sea. The Romans had made up their minds to carry the war into Africa; the Carthaginians strained every nerve to prevent this being done. Nowhere, they knew, would they fight at a greater disadvantage than at home. The native tribes which they ruled were hostile at heart, suffering as they did from oppression and tyranny. The presence of a Roman army would certainly be a signal for rebellion.

The Roman fleet numbered 330 ships of war, manned by crews of nearly 100,000 men in all. It carried an army of nearly 40,000. The Carthaginian fleet was even more numerous and had the advantage of not being encumbered with a land force. The plan of the Roman admirals was to break the enemy's line. Both consuls were present, each having a squadron of the swiftest and strongest ships. They were to make their way through the enemy; the rest of the fleet was to follow them.

The plan was not carried out in anything like completeness. The Carthaginians on the left of their battle-line made a feigned retreat, and the Roman ships on the right pursued, and lost touch of their comrades.

Meanwhile, the third and fourth divisions, those which intended to follow the advance of the consuls, were thrown into confusion by skilfully manœuvred attacks by the Carthaginian admirals. Nevertheless, the Romans won the day, and won it in the same way as at Mylæ. When it came to fighting at close quarters, there was no resisting them. When a Carthaginian ship was boarded, it was lost.

Sixty were taken in this way, but not a single Roman vessel suffered the same fate. In respect of ships sunk by ramming and in other ways, there was not much difference between the two, the Carthaginians lost thirty, and the Romans twenty-six. The immediate result of the victory was that an army was landed on the African coast.

Before I tell the story of this campaign, I will finish what has to be said about the Roman fleet. The victory of Ecnomus, for the battle described above is so named, was followed by great disasters. In the summer of 255 B.C. a fleet was sailing along the southern coast of Sicily when a fearful storm arose, and almost entirely wrecked about four-fifths of the ships. Another fleet was built, and some of the Carthaginian possessions on the Sicilian coast were taken. But of this, also, more than a half was lost by a second storm. This took place in 253 B.C.

The Romans were content for a while to borrow ships from their friend King Hiero of Syracuse. In 249 B.C., however, they had built another fleet, but only to lose three-fourths of it under the reckless mismanagement of the Consul Appius Claudius at the battle of

Drepana (*Trapani*). The fleet was again made up to a respectable force, only again to perish by a tempest in which every ship was wrecked—fortunately as many of the sailors were on shore, without any great loss of life.

The story told of this unlucky or incompetent commander is curiously characteristic of Roman ways of thinking. The Claudian family, though characterised for many generations by an ability which kept it steadily at the front, was eminently unpopular at Rome. It had an evil reputation for *incivilitas*, a word which we may translate by "aristocratic insolence." It is the habit of mind which despises the rules by which the *civis*, the citizen, should model his language and demeanour.

Appius Claudius conceived a bold design of destroying the Carthaginian fleet, as it lay in the harbour of Drepana. But he had not the knowledge and ability to carry it into execution. He arrived at the scene of action too late, got himself into trouble by delivering a rash attack, and had not the skill to recover himself. His countrymen attributed the disaster to his impiety.

A fleet on active service carried with it a number of chickens, from which the course of future events might be learnt (the cries and movements of all birds were supposed to be significant, but the habits of the domestic fowl made it peculiarly suitable for the purpose).

The *pullarius*,* as the keeper of these creatures was called, when the proper time was come, opened the cage and threw a certain kind of soft cake to the

---

* *Pullus* = a chicken: compare our "pullet."

birds. If they refused to come out of their hutch and eat, if they uttered a cry, if they fluttered their wings, if they tried to fly away, the signs were bad. If, on the other hand, they ate greedily, so greedily that morsels of the food fell to the earth, all promised well. The *pullarius* had reported to the consul that the chickens had refused to eat. The consul was not disposed to put up with the disappointment. "If they won't eat," he cried, "then at least they shall drink." And he ordered that they should be thrown into the sea.

Unfortunately, the ladies of the Claudian house were just as insolent as the men, and three years after this unlucky affair one of them more than justified their reputation. Her carriage was inconveniently delayed by a crowd as she was returning home from the public games. "How I wish," she cried, "that my brother could come to life again, and take command of another fleet! Then we should not have such crowds in the streets of Rome." The officials who were in charge of the games fined her for her audacious speech, which certainly showed the family characteristic of *incivilitas*.

That nothing was done for four years after this disaster need not surprise us; the wonder is that in 243 B.C. another fleet was built, largely at the expense of private citizens, the resources of the State being almost exhausted. Early in the following year it sailed, and met the Carthaginian force at Aegusa, an island on the western coast of Sicily. Carthage, believing that her enemy had definitely abandoned the sea, had suffered her fleet to fall into an ineffective condition, and the result of this battle was a complete victory for the Romans, who sank fifty and captured seventy of the enemy's ships. It was a magnificent effort and had the result which it deserved, for it practically ended the war. The whole of Sicily became virtually the possession of Rome, Hiero retaining Syracuse in reward for his steady loyalty.

Bust of Hannibal

The fate of Regulus is the second of the two incidents referred to in the beginning of this chapter. The result of the victory of Ecnomus had been that a Roman army had landed in Africa under the command of one of its consuls of the year, Atilius Regulus. His operations were very successful. The Carthaginian forces were utterly unable to hold the field against him. They lost all control over their native subjects, and by the beginning of the year 255 B.C. were besieged in their city. Regulus now offered conditions of peace. But these conditions were extremely severe. They amounted to a surrender of their whole Empire outside Africa. A compact to keep eight warships for the service of Rome, while they were to have but one for their own, and the payment of an annual tribute were the terms imposed.

The Carthaginians felt that it would be better to perish fighting, and their resolution met with its due reward. A Spartan officer of the name of Xanthippus had been engaged by one of the recruiting agents and now arrived. He criticised the military arrangements of the native generals with severity and gave an exhibition of his own tactical skill. He was put in supreme command, took the field, and inflicted a crushing defeat on the Roman army, taking a great number of prisoners, amongst whom was Regulus himself.

What was left of the Roman army quitted Africa, and the attempt to invade was not made again. For four years Regulus was kept in prison, in 251 B.C. he was sent to propose terms of peace on behalf of his captors.

What he did was to urge his countrymen to refuse the terms which were offered. If they held out, they would obtain much more favourable conditions. As for himself, he must not, he said, be considered. To make peace that he might be released from captivity would be monstrous. A man who had suffered the disgrace of capture should be left to perish. Wife, children, country were nothing to him now. He had lost them all. He put aside all attempts to detain him, returned to Carthage as he had taken oath to do, and died after suffering the most cruel tortures.

It was the indomitable energy of the nation and the patriotic self-sacrifice of the individual that decided the struggle between the two states.

CHAPTER X

THE CRITICAL STRUGGLE

THE twenty-three years that passed between the first Punic war and the second[1] were spent by Rome in making her position in Italy safe, especially in the northern portion, where the Ligurians, inhabiting the region now known as Piedmont, were conquered, and the Gauls much weakened. Colonies were planted and main roads constructed. The eastern shore of the Adriatic was also brought under Roman influence. Sardinia was acquired, though the tribes of the interior still remained practically independent.

It was a busy time, but there was a quiet interval in 235 B.C. when the temple of Janus[2] was shut for the second time in Roman history. Carthage suffered a great disaster at the beginning of this period. Her mercenary troops, whose pay was greatly in arrear, re-

[1] The wars with Carthage were known as the first, second and third Punic wars. The word had the same root as Phœnician.

[2] The gates of the temple of Janus stood open as long as there was war in any part of the world with which Rome was concerned. The God was supposed to have gone forth to help her armies. When there was peace, they were closed in order to keep the God at home. It is said to have happened three times in Roman history: in the peaceful reign of Numa, in the year mentioned above, and in the reign of Augustus.

volted, and were joined by the native tribes. The rebellion was at length put down, but at one time the city was in great danger. It was the same cause that brought about the loss of Sardinia. The mercenaries mutinied and put their Carthaginian officers to death. Unable, however, to hold their ground against the native tribes they asked Rome for help. Rome replied by taking possession of the island for herself.

In another direction, however, Carthage was more successful, establishing what seemed likely to be a permanent dominion in Spain. At the close of the first Punic war a young general, by name Hamilcar,[*] had distinguished himself by his brilliant defence of one of the last strongholds held by Carthage. He felt, and not without reason, that his abilities had not had a fair field. The hope and aim of his life was to restore the fortunes of his country. Spain was the field which he chose for this purpose; it was, indeed, the only one that was open to him.

He crossed over to it in 238 B.C. and spent there the remaining nine years of his life. In 229 B.C. he fell in an encounter with a plundering tribe which he had set out to punish. His son-in-law Hasdrubal took up his work, and carried it on with success for eight years. At the end of this time he was assassinated by a slave whose master he had put to death.

Hasdrubal had for some time been assisted by a very able second-in-command, a son of Hamilcar, Hannibal by name, who was destined to be the most

---

[*] He was distinguished by the surname of Barcas *(lightning)*. So we have *Barak* and *Boanerges*.

formidable of the enemies whom Rome was called upon to encounter. He had been brought up from childhood to hate the Roman name. His father, when about to sail for Spain, was offering the usual sacrifices, and Hannibal, then a boy of nine, was standing near—he told the story himself in after years—"Would you go with me into Spain?" asked Hamilcar. The child, of course, assented with delight. "Then lay your hand upon the altar, and swear that you will never be the friend of Rome."

He grew up a child of the camp, and never was there a youth who took more kindly to the soldier's life. "Bold in the extreme in meeting peril he was perfectly cool in its presence. No toil could weary his body or conquer his spirit. Heat and cold he bore with equal endurance. The cravings of nature, not the pleasure of the palate, determined the measure of his food and drink. His waking or sleeping hours were not regulated by day or night. Such time as his work left him he gave to repose; but it was not on a soft couch or in stillness that he sought it. Many a man often saw him wrapped in his military cloak, lying on the ground amid the sentries and pickets. His dress was not in any way better than those of his comrades, but his arms and horses were splendid. And as he was the first to enter the battle so he was the last to leave it."

Such is Livy's picture of the man. He was a professional soldier of the very finest type, and the Roman amateurs were unfitted to meet him. But the amateurs of a nation of warriors learn their business in time, and learn it well. How much progress was made in the twenty years thus spent in bringing Spain under Carthaginian rule, we do not know. The effort would not have been persisted in so long if it had not met with a satisfactory success; that the success was not complete we may be sure. One considerable region remained independent for two centuries more. It was not before the latter half of the first century B.C. that the Cantabri (the Basques of modern times) submitted to Rome.

The Carthaginian progress, we know, attracted the notice of the Roman Government, and an agreement was arranged with Hannibal that no military operations should be carried on North of the Ebro.

The formal breach between the two powers came in 219 B.C. After a skilful attack and an obstinate defence which made the siege one of the most memorable in history, Hannibal took the town of Saguntum.[*] It was a disputed point whether Saguntum had been included in the agreement made with Hasdrubal—it lay about a hundred miles south of the Ebro—but Hannibal felt that to attack it would be to challenge Rome, and he delayed till his plans were complete. Envoys were sent to remonstrate with him while the siege was in progress. He refused to listen to them. Nothing further had been done when tidings reached Rome that Saguntum had fallen.

Then at last the government acted. They sent an embassy to Carthage demanding that Hannibal and his principal officers and the leaders of the party in the Senate which had supported him should be given up.

---

[*] Now Murviedro, a name derived from *muri veteres*, the old walls, which long remained to testify the former features of the city.

It was an outrageous demand, made, one would think, that it might be refused. Refused, of course, it was. After a long and heated argument, Fabius Maximus, of whom we shall hear again, stood up. He pointed to the ample folds of the gown *(toga)* which he wore and said: "Here I carry peace and war, which will you have?" "That which you choose to give," answered the President of the Senate. Then said Fabius, "I give you war."

One of the objections to what we may call popular government is to be seen in the Roman policy. There is sure to be a conflict of opinions about public policy, sometimes there are divergent interests, and the result is slow and hesitating action, sharply contrasting with the vigour and promptitude with which a single mind and will arrives at conclusions and acts upon them. No one at Rome, it would seem, saw the position of affairs truly, or had any idea of the turn which the war would take. That the wonderful genius of Hannibal should not have been discerned is not surprising. It is the way of such men to take the world by surprise.

The Roman statesmen had no other idea but that the war would be fought out in Spain; Hannibal, however, had determined to invade Italy. He had much to do, though, before he could carry out his plan. Saguntum had fallen, it is probable, in the late summer of 219 B.C., and it was not before the autumn of 218 B.C. that Hannibal arrived at the foot of the Alps. The time had been fully occupied. He had reduced the country between the Ebro and the Pyrenees to at least outward submission, had made provision for defending Africa, and, leaving Spain, had made his way over the Pyrenees, and forced the passage of the Rhone.

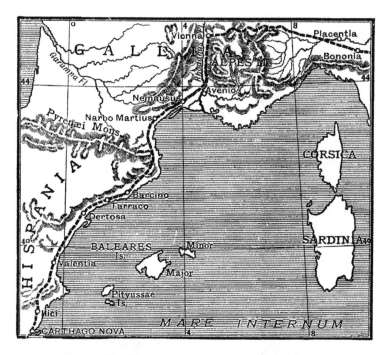

Hannibal's route across the Alps.

Doubtless it would have been impossible to do so much in a shorter space of time. It is a fact, however, that the necessary delays gave the Roman Government a chance which it failed to make use of.

One notable example is to be found in the passage of the Rhone. It was only with the opposition of the native tribes that Hannibal had to deal. The Romans must have known that Hannibal's route would be in this direction, and it seems evident that if their

"The passage of the Alps was effected
under many difficulties."

army had been at hand to assist the defence, the invaders might have been driven back. Scipio, the general in command of the Roman force, arrived at the river four days late. It is one of the gifts of a great general to calculate correctly the probable action of his opponents, and this Hannibal seems to have possessed in the highest degree.

Bust of Scipio

The passage of the Alps was effected under many difficulties. There were hostile tribes, there was no well-defined track to be followed, and the season was dangerously late. But Rome made no effort to bar the way or to attack Hannibal's army before it had recovered from the fatigues of the passage. That these and the losses which followed them were exceedingly severe cannot be doubted.

Numbers are always doubtful, but Livy relates, on the authority of a Roman soldier who was taken prisoner by the Carthaginians, that, with the addition of a number of recruits from the tribes on the Italian side of the Alps, the army numbered 80,000 infantry and 10,000 cavalry, and that Hannibal estimated his own loss in the passage of the Alps at 36,000 men. Some writers declared that the invading force only numbered 20,000 infantry and 6,000 cavalry when it reached Italy.

This is scarcely to be believed, but it can hardly be doubted that if Rome had acted quickly and with vigour the enemy might have been crushed at once. But again Hannibal knew with whom he was dealing, and his action was justified by the result.

CHAPTER XI

THE CRITICAL STRUGGLE
(continued)

THE war which followed Hannibal's descent into Italy lasted for sixteen years (218-202 B.C.).

For three years Rome was in great danger. Then, for a while, the armies fought on equal terms, though to us, at least, it is quite evident that Hannibal's great effort was not going to succeed. Then the fortunes of Carthage began to decline, till in 207 B.C. occurred disasters which implied their ultimate ruin. For the five years that followed Hannibal carried on a hopeless struggle with an ingenuity and courage which no one else could have shown.

In the few weeks that intervened between the arrival of Hannibal in Italy and the retirement of the opposing armies into winter quarters, the Romans suffered two reverses. The first engagement (at the Ticinus) was nothing more than a cavalry skirmish, the second (at the Trebia) was a more serious affair. The generals were out-manœuvred, and the troops were not good enough to make up for the incompetence of their commanders. The camp was taken, and the survivors had to take refuge in the fortified towns of Placentia and Cremona: a more serious result was that all the Italian Gauls declared for Carthage.

Another weakness in the Roman system was now revealed, and not for the first time. The consuls for the year 217 B.C. came into office in March. One of them, Flaminius, owed his election, if Livy is to be trusted, to political reasons. He was certainly an incompetent commander. Hannibal was greatly weakened by losses suffered in a march through the marshes of the Arno, but no advantage was taken of the opportunity by the Romans.

When Hannibal was sufficiently recruited he contrived by skilful strategy to draw the Romans into a trap. Flaminius, anxious, as we may suppose, not to lose any time, started in pursuit of Hannibal, who had marched southward. His shortest way was along the shores of Lake Trasimene, and he followed it without making any attempt to reconnoitre. On this road he encamped for the night. Hannibal had put a strong force in ambush on the hills which commanded the road, and both the entrance into the valley and the exit from it were held in force.

The result was the almost total destruction of the Roman Army. Out of 40,000 only 10,000 found their way to Rome; many lay dead on the field of battle, the consul, who had done his best to retrieve the disaster, among them. Fifteen thousand prisoners remained in Hannibal's hands.

A greater disaster was to follow, and it would seem from the same cause. The first elected of the two consuls for the year 216 B.C., was a certain Terentius Varro,[1] and here again the choice was dictated, not by military, but by political reasons. Varro was the son of a butcher, who had made himself popular by supporting democratic measures. Hannibal was now in Southern Italy, and the two consuls marched to meet him, with urgent instructions to fight.

It is clear that there were two parties in Rome, one calling for speedy action, the other, represented by Q. Fabius Maximus, who had been made Dictator after the disaster of Trasimene, insisting on a policy of caution. The former party was now the stronger.

And in the camp the consuls were nearly as much divided as at home. It was a bad custom, though quite in accord with the way in which such things were managed in Rome, that when both consuls were present with the army they commanded on alternate days. Varro forced a skirmish on one of his days and gained a slight advantage. After this delay was out of the question. Æmilius did all that he could to safeguard the position, but Varro, who had had no military experience, was resolved on action.

In the early morning of August 2nd, 216,[2] he crossed the river on the further bank of which part of the Roman army had already encamped. The battle opened with a Roman success. The legions in the cen-

---

[1] No other candidate obtained a majority of votes, and consequently a second election had to be held, Varro, of course, presiding. At the second election a distinguished general, Æmilius Paullus by name, was chosen.

[2] The real date was much earlier in the year, the calendar being greatly in error.

tre broke the line of the Gallic and Spanish infantry which faced them. They followed up the flying foe too far, a mistake of which they soon became aware, but not soon enough. The African infantry from the two wings closed in upon them, and were followed by the Carthaginian horse, which had by this time routed the very inferior cavalry opposed to them. In a very short time the battle was hopelessly lost.

The army was almost cut to pieces. One of the consuls perished on the field. Livy tells a pathetic story of how a Roman horseman saw him sitting on a stone, and offered to carry him to a place of safety. "Suffer me," cried Æmilius, "to die amidst my slaughtered comrades. Do you save yourself." Varro escaped with a company of less than a hundred horsemen. It seemed as if the ruin of Rome was complete.

And now the noble strength of a free people came out. It refused to abandon itself to despair. The Senate took the lead. Varro was odious to it in every way, a demagogue whose foolish rashness had brought the State to the brink of ruin, but they solemnly thanked him because he had not despaired of his country.

A company of young nobles who had meditated flight from Italy were forcibly detained and encouraged to stand by their country to the last. Everyone that was of military age was enrolled in the ranks; even criminals were not rejected, and slaves were trusted with arms.

It has often been asked why Hannibal did not at once march on Rome. His own officers are said to have reproached him with his want of energy—"You know how to win a victory," said one of them, "but not how to use it." Probably he was a better judge of the situation than anyone else. When he did make an advance on the city five years afterwards, he gained nothing by the movement. The story was that the very spot on which he was encamped was sold in Rome at the very time of its occupation and fetched its full price.

One thing is quite certain, that, as Mommsen puts it, "the gradual decline of Hannibal's power dates really from his victory at Cannæ." If he could not bring the struggle to an end after so complete a victory, he was not likely to do so at all.

Five years afterwards Carthage suffered the reverse which made obvious to all that the policy of attacking Rome in Italy had failed.

Rome, indeed, recovered herself with amazing rapidity. Two years had scarcely passed when she felt herself strong enough to assume the aggressive. Hannibal was still in Italy with his strength practically unbroken, with many of the native tribes in alliance with him, and more ready to join him if the opportunity should present itself, and yet the Romans boldly transferred a large part of their force to Sicily. Their old friend, King Hiero, died early in 215. His grandson and successor, Hieronymus, repudiated their alliance. Little more than a year afterwards he was assassinated, and a republic was substituted for the monarchy. The new rulers, however, were not less hostile to Rome. Action became necessary if Sicily was not to be wholly lost, and Marcellus in the spring of 214 undertook the siege of Syracuse. This was a very formidable enterprise. Some two hundred years before Athens had brought ruin upon herself by attempting it. It might well have seemed the extreme of rashness when Rome, with Hannibal, so to speak, at her gates, attempted the task which Athens with her undivided forces had failed to perform.

Marcellus began by trying active measures, but the city was extraordinarily strong, thanks to its natural position and to its elaborate fortifications. The defenders, too, could command the services of the greatest mechanician of antiquity, the famous Archimedes. Every effort of the besiegers was baffled; showers of stones and javelins from the catapults cleared the decks of their ships, and the ships themselves were seized by huge grappling irons and overturned. Then a blockade was tried; but Marcellus had not the force to make it effective. He then resolved to attack the city from the land side; and having discovered a weak spot in the fortifications, took the occasion of a city festival to deliver an attack. One portion of the city fell into his hands; the other two made but a feeble resistance, and Syracuse was gained, and the soldiers were permitted to plunder the city, but were forbidden to injure the inhabitants. The great Archimedes, however, perished, much to the grief of the Roman general. A soldier forced his way into his room, could not rouse him from the study of some mathematical problem with which he was engaged, and cut him down. Before the year had come to an end, all Sicily, with the single exception of Agrigentum *(Girgenti)* had submitted to Rome. It was an act of magnificent courage.

It is difficult, if not impossible, to find a parallel in history, ancient or modern; but we may form some idea of what it meant if we suppose that the British government, after sustaining on English soil a defeat more disastrous than that which Napoleon suffered at Waterloo, with an enemy in possession of Dorset, Somersetshire, Devonshire, and Cornwall, with the Irish ready to rise in revolt, should despatch half its available force for the conquest of the Netherlands.

But there was something in the conduct of the Roman commander which was ominous of future evil. Marcellus was personally incorruptible; but he stripped Syracuse of its treasures of art. These were intended to adorn his triumph, an honour which was not given to him, and then to be deposited in two temples which he had vowed to build. The religious motive doubtless seemed to excuse the act. But it was a bad precedent. The temples were the picture galleries of Rome. Practically the city was enriched by the spoils of Syracuse. And it was an easy step from temples to private houses. It became the practice for Roman nobles to adorn their mansions with works of art carried away from conquered cities. The death of Marcellus before he could find an opportunity of dedicating the temples was regarded as a judgment on his impiety.

Hannibal had left his brother Hasdrubal in Spain in charge of the interests of Carthage in that country. Here he had lost much ground; we may be sure that such reinforcements as were to be spared had gone to Italy rather than to the less important field of action. Still he had a considerable force at his disposal, and Hannibal saw that the only chance that remained to him was to summon this to his help.

The march was effected with very little loss, though it certainly took a long time. Hasdrubal crossed the Pyrenees in the autumn of 209 B.C., spent the following year in Gaul, doubtless in gathering recuits for his army, and crossed in the spring of 207 B.C.

The Roman authorities, though they could hardly have been ignorant of his purpose, had made no preparations to meet him. But this neglect was repaired by the energy of the men who were in command of the armies in the field.

Hasdrubal himself lost some of the advantage which had fallen to him. His best plan, as far as we are able to judge, would have been to lose no time in effecting a junction with Hannibal; what he did was to lay siege to Placentia *(Piacenza)*, hoping, we may suppose, to find there some of the supplies which he needed. The siege failed and he resolved to march southward, sending four mounted Gauls to announce his purpose to Hannibal, and to arrange for a junction of the two armies. The Gauls lost their way, fell into the hands of the Romans, and were compelled to give up the despatch which they carried.

Claudius Nero, who was watching Hannibal, took a bold resolve. He left his camp in charge of his second-in-command, and marched northward with a picked force of 7,000 men to reinforce the consul Livius, who was by this time facing Hasdrubal in

Northern Italy. He effected the junction without meeting with any mishap, and the two consuls resolved to give battle at once.

But Hasdrubal, a veteran who had had many years' experience in the field, and who knew something about Roman ways, had at least some suspicion of the truth. His scouts had observed in the enemies' watering parties men and horses that bore marks of a recent journey, and he noticed that the trumpets sounded twice in the Roman camp, showing that both the consuls were present. He left his position, and marched, probably with the intention of joining his brother, but his guide deceived him, he lost his way, and found himself compelled to give battle. The place was the left bank of the river Metaurus, a name which was thenceforward to be famous in Roman history.

The battle which followed was stubbornly fought. Hasdrubal did all that skill and courage could suggest, but his army was inferior in number to his enemy, and though some of his troops were of excellent quality his new recruits were worth but little. His elephants did at least as much harm to their own side as to the enemy, and the Gauls made but a feeble resistance to the charge which, though Hasdrubal had been careful to put them in the strongest available position, the Romans contrived to deliver.

The Carthaginian loss was heavy. Hasdrubal fell fighting in the midst of the Roman line; he had no wish to survive the ruin of his hopes. The greater part of his army, it is true, made its escape, but they were not fighting for their country, and they never cared again to face the conquerors in the field. Nero started the same night for his command in the south, carrying with him the head of Hasdrubal, which he is said to have thrown into Hannibal's camp.

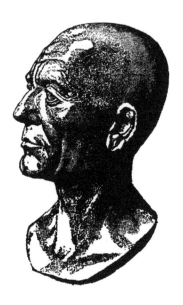

The Younger Scipio.

In 203 B.C. Hannibal left Italy, where he had for some time been keeping up a hopeless resistance to the Roman army. In the following year the final battle of the war was fought at Zama *(Jama)*, and ended in a defeat so disastrous that nothing was left for Carthage but to make peace on such conditions as Rome was willing to grant. These were not as severe as might have been expected.

Carthage retained her independence, but she ceased to be a rival of Rome. Her actual end was delayed for more than fifty years, but the sobering effects of her rivalry now ceased to work.

A great Roman historian puts down to this cause the country's debasement. "Those who had lightly borne toils and dangers, doubtful fortunes and desperate straits, found leisure and wealth a pitiable burden. At first the lust of money, then the lust for power increased, and these were the source of every evil."

It was, perhaps, the thought of what might come to pass in the future that troubled the mind of one of Rome's noblest sons, the Younger Scipio. Carthage, after a desperate resistance, had fallen into his hands and had been given up to plunder. This seemed to him punishment enough. But there came to him an express command from the authorities at Rome that the city and its suburbs should be entirely destroyed, its site ploughed up, and a solemn curse pronounced on anyone who should attempt to rebuild it. Scipio knew perfectly well that as a rival power Carthage had ceased to exist, that the motive for this monstrous decree was commercial jealousy, the same base cupidity which in the very same year was to bring the same fate on Corinth. He turned to his old friend and teacher, Polybius—it is Polybius who tells the story—and said: "O Polybius, this is a great deed, but I shudder to think that some day a conqueror may pass the same doom on Rome." And as the fire raged—it lasted, the same authority tells us, seventeen days—he murmured the lines of Homer:—

"The day wherein Ilium the holy shall perish will come;
    it is near
Unto Priam withal, and the folk of the king of the
    ashen spear."

The dominions of Rome were yet to increase for more than three centuries.[*]

She was yet to produce great soldiers, great statesmen, even great patriots; but it was not for the noblest of her sons that place and power were reserved. The lessons that we learn from her history are thenceforward of what we should avoid rather than of what we should imitate.

[*] The last acquisition was that of Dacia, conquered by Trajan in 107 A.D. Dacia was bounded on the north by the Carpathians, and on the east by Hierasus, a river which flows into the Danube at Galatz.

CPSIA information can be obtained
at www.ICGtesting.com
Printed in the USA
BVHW08s2021020918
526275BV00003B/29/P